W9-BSS-726

IF YOU WERE A KID ABOARD THE

Titanic

BY JOSH GREGORY • ILLUSTRATED BY SEBASTIÀ SERRA

CHILDREN'S PRESS®
An Imprint of Scholastic Inc.

Content Consultant
James Marten, PhD, Professor and Chair, History Department, Marquette University, Milwaukee, Wisconsin

NOTE TO THE READER, PARENT, LIBRARIAN, AND TEACHER: This book combines a historical fiction
narrative with nonfiction fact boxes. While all the nonfiction fact boxes are historically accurate
and true, the fiction comes solely from the imaginations of the author and illustrator.

Photos ©: 9: JT Vintage/age fotostock; 11: Krista Few/Ralph White/Corbis/Getty Images; 13: David Paul Morris/
Getty Images; 15: Charly Triballeau/AFP/Getty Images; 17: Universal Images Group/age fotostock; 19: Oskari
Porkka/Thinkstock; 21 top: Richard Schlecht/Getty Images; 21 bottom: UniversalImagesGroup/Getty Images; 23:
World History Archive/age fotostock; 25: Ralph White/Getty Images; 27: Ralph White/Getty Images.

Library of Congress Cataloging-in-Publication Data
Names: Gregory, Josh, author. | Serra, Sebastià, 1966– illustrator.
Title: If you were a kid aboard the Titanic / by Josh Gregory ; illustrated by Sebastià Serra.
Description: New York : Children's Press, an Imprint of Scholastic Inc., 2017. | Series: If You Were a Kid |
    Includes bibliographical references and index.
Identifiers: LCCN 2016038597| ISBN 9780531223826 (library binding) | ISBN 9780531230961 (paperback)
Subjects: LCSH: Titanic (Steamship)—History—Juvenile literature. | Ocean travel—early 20th century—
    Juvenile literature.
Classification: LCC G530.T6 G73 2017 | DDC 910.9163/4—dc23
LC record available at https://lccn.loc.gov/2016038597

No part of this publication may be reproduced in whole or in part, or stored in a retrieval system, or transmitted in any form or by any
means, electronic, mechanical, photocopying, recording, or otherwise, without written permission of the publisher. For information regarding
permission, write to Scholastic Inc., Attention: Permissions Department, 557 Broadway, New York, NY 10012.
© 2017 Scholastic Inc.

All rights reserved. Published in 2017 by Children's Press, an imprint of Scholastic Inc.
Printed in the United States of America 113
SCHOLASTIC, CHILDREN'S PRESS, and associated logos are trademarks and/or registered trademarks of Scholastic Inc.
1 2 3 4 5 6 7 8 9 10 R 26 25 24 23 22 21 20 19 18 17

TABLE OF CONTENTS

TITANIC

A Different Way of Life

On April 10, 1912, a ship called the RMS *Titanic* set off from its harbor in Southampton, England, on its first voyage. After picking up additional passengers in France and Ireland, the *Titanic* began the journey across the Atlantic Ocean to New York City. The thousands of people aboard couldn't have imagined the disaster that waited ahead. Imagine you were a kid aboard the *Titanic*. The trip to New York was scheduled to take about a week. During that time, the *Titanic* would be your home. You would eat your meals, bathe, and sleep on the ship. You would also have plenty of time to have fun with friends and family. You might even meet some interesting new people.

Turn the page to begin your own voyage aboard the *Titanic*! You will see that life today is a lot different than it was in the past.

Meet Alice!

Alice Carver has lived in England all her life. But things have been tough since her father died two years ago. Alice and her mother are moving to America to live with relatives. They don't have a lot of money, so they had to buy the cheapest tickets for the *Titanic*'s voyage. Alice's mom said that means they have to stay in the bottom of the ship. But Alice has other plans. She is sure she'll find a way to see the rest of the ship. . . .

Meet William!

William Alexander III comes from a very wealthy British family. His parents bought tickets for one of the finest **suites** on the *Titanic* simply to experience the great ship's first voyage. It will be William's first time making such a long trip across the ocean, and he is a little scared. Everyone says the *Titanic* is almost unsinkable, but he is worried anyway. Worse yet, William's older cousin George is coming, too. George always teases William and makes him feel bad. . . .

7

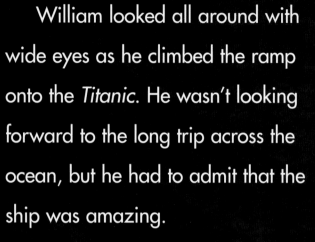

William looked all around with wide eyes as he climbed the ramp onto the *Titanic*. He wasn't looking forward to the long trip across the ocean, but he had to admit that the ship was amazing.

Suddenly, someone pushed him from behind. "Keep moving!" shouted his cousin George. "Unless you're too scared, that is."

William sighed and kept walking up the ramp. Why did George have to be so annoying?

A REMARKABLE SHIP

If you wanted to cross the ocean in the early 1900s, you had to go by ship. To make the long voyage more comfortable, companies built better and better ships. The *Titanic* was expected to be one of the biggest and best of its time. People around the world followed news of its construction.

The *Titanic* was operated by a company called White Star Line.

FOR PASSENGER TRAFFIC ONLY 40 FT

As soon as she was on board, Alice was ready to explore. It was her first time on a ship. She wanted to see everything.

"Don't go too far," her mom said as she unpacked in their cramped third-class room. But Alice was already out the door and skipping down the hallway. There were lots of people moving around the ship. Alice realized that this was a good chance to sneak into the first- and second-class areas.

FIRST, SECOND, AND THIRD CLASS

On the *Titanic*, you would be in one of three classes depending on your ticket. First-class tickets were the most expensive. If you were in first class, you would be able to see the ship's most impressive areas. Third-class tickets were the cheapest. If you were in this class, you would be limited to a small part of the ship. You would not be allowed to enter the most amazing spaces of the *Titanic*.

Passengers stroll along the deck of the *Titanic*.

11

William was also out of his room. George had been bothering him all day. Taking a walk was the only way to get away. But his walk wasn't as peaceful as he planned. Suddenly, a girl came running around the corner and crashed into him.

A crew member was chasing after her. "You can't be here!" he shouted. William thought quickly. "It's OK," he said. "This is my sister."

THE FINEST ROOMS

A first-class suite on the *Titanic* was extremely expensive and only affordable for very rich people. It would cost thousands of dollars in today's money. A suite included your own bathroom and rooms for getting dressed. The entire suite was decorated in the finest furniture. First-class suites were also located on the parts of the ship where you wouldn't feel the ocean's movement as much.

The *Titanic*'s first-class rooms looked like this.

"Thanks," Alice said as
the crew member walked away.
"I almost got caught!"

The two introduced
themselves. "Why was he
chasing you?" asked William.

"I'm in third class," Alice
said. "But I really wanted to
see the rest of the ship."

William smiled. "I think
I can help you out!"

LIFE IN THIRD CLASS

If you had a third-class ticket on the *Titanic*, you would share a small room with up to five other people. You would sleep on a bunk bed. You would also share a bathroom with other travelers. But third-class rooms were still very nice. They all had running water and electricity. You probably wouldn't have had these things in your home if you were a third-class passenger.

The *Titanic's* third-class rooms looked like this.

Glad to spend time away from George, William helped Alice explore the *Titanic* over the next few days. Alice wasn't supposed to be in first class. But as long as they were together, no one would suspect her of being out of place.

The two new friends walked up a huge staircase made of beautiful carved wood. They went for a swim in the ship's pool. They played games outside on the **deck**. They even listened to an **orchestra** play music.

FUN ABOARD

You would have many ways to stay busy on board the *Titanic*. In first class you could exercise or play sports in a gym. You could also enjoy cafés and restaurants. In third class, you might gather in a place called the general room. There people talked and played games. You might also have enjoyed visiting the ship's decks for ocean views.

A woman rides an exercise bike in the *Titanic*'s gym.

On the fifth night aboard the *Titanic*, Alice was sleeping peacefully above her mother in their room. Suddenly, she was jolted awake as she felt the ship shake. Other people on the ship began to wake up, too.

Eventually, crew members started knocking on cabin doors. They told people on the ship to go to the decks and get ready to **board** lifeboats. Alice started to worry. What was happening?

A DEADLY CRASH

On the night of April 14, 1912, the *Titanic* was damaged when it ran into an **iceberg** floating in the water. The iceberg tore holes along the side of the ship. Water began pouring inside. Depending on where you were on the ship, you might not have known anything was wrong. Some people noticed right away.

Only a portion of an iceberg sticks out above the water's surface. The underwater part is often even bigger!

In first class, William and his family started making their way toward the deck. Some people nearby were laughing and joking. They didn't think anything was wrong. But William knew that his worst fear had come true. The ship was sinking. He thought about Alice down in third class. It was so far away. Would she be able to make it to the lifeboats in time? He needed to find her.

A REALLY BIG VESSEL

The *Titanic* was a very big ship. It also had many different levels. This meant that it could take someone a long time to travel from one part of the ship to another. As a result, many people in third class had a hard time reaching the ship's lifeboats in time.

92.5 feet (28.2 meters) wide

882.5 feet (269 m) long

Alice and her mom were trying to get to the lifeboats, but the third-class area was very crowded. It was hard to move. Luckily, Alice knew a shortcut from sneaking into the other parts of the ship. "Mom, follow me!" she said.

As they were making their way through the ship, Alice turned a corner and ran face-first into a young boy.

A LACK OF LIFEBOATS

One reason so many people died on the *Titanic* is that there weren't enough lifeboats. The ship's 20 lifeboats could only hold 1,178 people. That meant more than 1,000 people simply couldn't fit. To make matters worse, many lifeboats left in a hurry before they were full.

Titanic survivors paddle to safety in a lifeboat.

"William!" Alice yelled in surprise. "What are you doing here?"

"I was looking for you," William answered. "Come on!"

They ran to the deck. People all around were starting to panic. William's family was looking around for a lifeboat. "What are we going to do?" George asked. He had tears in his eyes.

"Over here!" William said. "There's plenty of room in this boat."

A TRAGIC END

Many people never made it off the *Titanic*. About 2,200 passengers and crewmembers were aboard the ship. However, only about 700 survived when the ship sank. If you were in first class, you had the best chance of making it onto a lifeboat. Most people in third class were not so lucky.

A bag and other objects left behind by the *Titanic's* passengers

As they floated in the lifeboat, everyone looked back toward the ship.
Their hearts ached as it broke in half and slowly sank into the ocean.
About an hour later, a large ship arrived and brought everyone aboard.
Alice was freezing cold, but happy to finally be out of the lifeboat.

"I guess you're braver than I thought," George said to William.

"Maybe," William replied as he and Alice exchanged a smile. "But right now I just want to get back on land."

73 YEARS LATER ◆ ◆ ◆

The *Titanic* was hidden on the ocean floor for many decades. Finally, in 1985, ocean explorers discovered the wreck. Since then, experts have studied it in detail. They have brought back many items that once belonged to the *Titanic*'s passengers. They have even brought back pieces of the ship itself. This has helped us learn more about what it was like to be on the *Titanic*.

Explorers took many photos showing how the *Titanic* had changed after decades underwater.

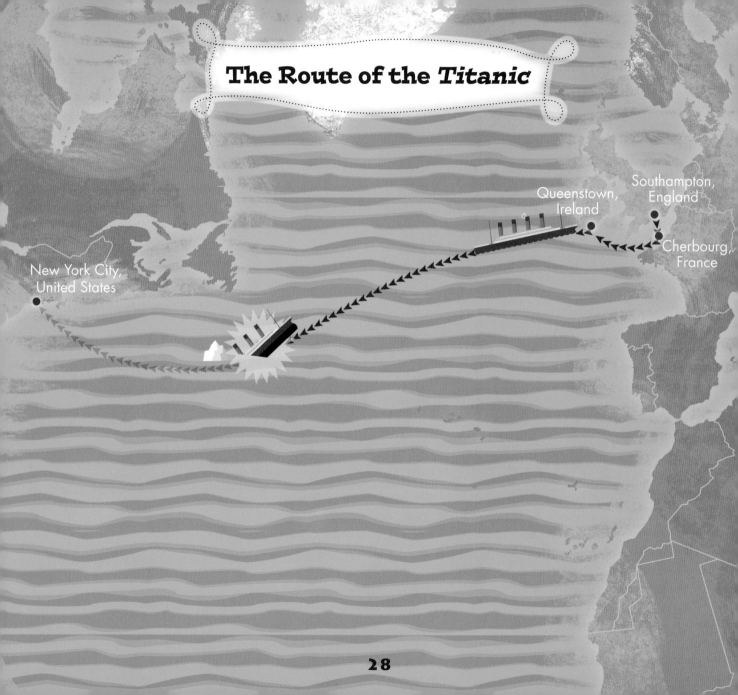

The Route of the Titanic

Queenstown, Ireland

Southampton, England

Cherbourg, France

New York City, United States

Timeline

1909   Construction of the *Titanic* begins in Ireland.

May 31, 1911   About 100,000 people watch as the *Titanic* is put in water for the first time.

April 10, 1912   The *Titanic* sets off on its voyage from Southampton, England.

April 14, 1912   The *Titanic* collides with an iceberg in the middle of the night and soon sinks.

September 1, 1985   A team of researchers discovers the wreck of the *Titanic*.

Words to Know

board (BORD) to get on or enter a ship, aircraft, or other vehicle

deck (DEK) the floor of a boat or ship

iceberg (ISE-burg) a large mass of ice that has broken off from a glacier and is floating in the sea

orchestra (OR-kuh-struh) an often large group of musicians who play a variety of musical instruments together

suites (SWEETZ) groups of rooms that are connected

Index

ABOUT THE AUTHOR

Josh Gregory is the author of more than 90 books for kids. He has written about everything from animals to technology to history. A graduate of the University of Missouri–Columbia, he currently lives in Portland, Oregon.

Visit this Scholastic Web site for more information about the *Titanic*:

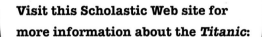

www.factsfornow.scholastic.com

Enter the keyword **Titanic**

ABOUT THE ILLUSTRATOR

Sebastià Serra was born in Barcelona, Spain. When he turned three, he received a pencil box for his birthday, and since then he has never stopped drawing. He has illustrated more than 100 books, and he has also worked for magazines, television, and theater. He has even won some prizes!